WHEN TWO OR MORE ARE GATHERED

FROM GRIEF TO GRACE

*An Anthology Written by
Eight Beautiful Women
Who Conquered Grief &
Were Empowered by Grace*

When Two Or More Are Gathered: From Grief to Grace

© 2024 Kimberly Peterson

Printed in the USA

ISBN (Print Version): ISBN- 9798323119349

All Rights Reserved. This book is protected by the copyright laws of the United States of America. This book may not be copied or reprinted for commercial gain or profit. The use of short quotations is permitted. Permission will be granted upon request. The author guarantees all contents are original and do not infringe upon the legal rights of any other person or work.

Cover: Destiny Premier Services

Publisher: Shekinah Glory Publishing

www.destinypremierservices.com

Dedication

This book is dedicated to those whom we shared life and love with but are now resting in peace.

Contents

Introduction 9

Kimberly Peterson 15
I Was Just Beginning

Ashley Arrington 31
From Grief to Grace

LaTeshia Bailey 45
Daddy's Not So Little Girl

Simone Gooden 59
Grieving Gracefully

Natarsha Hackney 75
Until The Last Breath

Lisa Johnson 87
Death By Suicide

Kayla P. Nimer 101
It Was Necessary

Kritina Mock-Palmer 113
From Pain to Purpose

Meet The Authors 127

Introduction

But he said to me, "My grace is sufficient for you, for my power is made perfect in weakness."

2 Corinthians 12:9a

Grief is a powerful and complex emotion that we all experience at some point in our lives. It is a natural response to loss, whether it be the loss of a loved one, a job, a dream, or any other significant change. Grieving is a process that looks different for everyone and there is no right or wrong way to grieve.

During times of grief, it is important to be gentle with ourselves and allow ourselves to feel and process our emotions. It is okay to seek support from friends, family, or a therapist to help navigate through the pain. Remember that healing takes time and it's okay to not be okay.

As we move through the stages of grief, it is important to remember that it is a journey towards acceptance and healing. While the pain may never fully go away, it will soften with time, and we can learn to carry our grief with us as we continue to live our lives. Through the process of grief, we can learn more about ourselves, our strengths, and our capacity for resilience.

The loss of a loved one is an experience that profoundly changes us, marking a before and after in the timeline of our lives. It is a journey through grief that is as personal as it is universal, touching upon the deepest emotions and questions about existence, love, and the nature of connection. The initial shock and disbelief give way to a myriad of emotions, ranging from profound sadness and longing to, at times, anger and confusion. This emotional turmoil reflects the depth and complexity of human bonds, highlighting how deeply another's life is intertwined with our own.

Navigating through grief is often described as moving through stages, but it's important to recognize that these stages are not linear nor prescriptive. Everyone experiences grief in their own unique way, and the process can involve a fluctuating mix of denial, anger, bargaining, depression, and acceptance. Essential to this journey is allowing oneself the space and permission to grieve, understanding that it is not a process that can be rushed or neatly concluded.

The support of friends, family, or a professional can provide a crucial lifeline during these times, offering a mirror to our experiences and feelings, and helping us to not feel so isolated in our pain.

Ultimately, the loss of a loved one reshapes our understanding of life and our place within it. It can lead to a deeper appreciation of our relationships and the preciousness of the time we have. Many find that with time, the sharp edges of pain dull, making way for memories that bring more comfort than sadness.

The process of integrating loss into our lives is a profound journey of transformation, leading to new insights about love, resilience, and the human spirit. In honoring our grief, we honor the ones we have lost, carrying forward their memory and the love we shared in ways that continue to influence our lives and the world around us.

Healing from the death of a loved one is a journey, both deeply personal and universally understood. It's a process that doesn't adhere to a strict timeline or set of rules, but rather meanders through the heart and soul, touching each individual differently. At the core of this healing journey is the understanding that grief is not something to be "fixed" or hurried along, but rather experienced and honored in its own time.

One of the keys to learning to live after loss is allowing oneself to feel the full spectrum of emotions without judgment. Grief can manifest in many forms, such as sadness, guilt, fear, or even relief, depending on the circumstances of the loss. It's important to give yourself permission to grieve and understand that it's a sign of love and connection that you had with the person who has passed.

As time progresses, finding ways to honor the memory of the loved one can be a healing part of the process. This could be through creating a memorial, engaging in activities they enjoyed, or volunteering for causes they cared about. Additionally, finding new hobbies, interests, or routines can help in slowly rebuilding a life that feels meaningful. It's also essential to be patient with yourself and acknowledge that healing takes time.

There will be good days and bad days, and that's perfectly normal. The loss will always be a part of you, but it doesn't have to define your entire existence. "When Two Or More Are Gathered: From Grief to

Grace" is a collection of real-life stories about the gripping realities of loss, that led to eight women experiencing God's amazing saving grace. If you have dealt with or are currently dealing with loss, this book will aid you on your journey to total healing, wholeness, and happiness. Each story will testify to the glory of God and how He brought them through in unique and empowering ways.

Kimberly Peterson

"I Was Just Beginning"

Recently, in an Instagram reel, a pastor was preaching a sermon, and he proposed the question to the congregation "Have you ever believed for something to live and had to watch it die?' I can truly relate! I lost my mom at the tender age of twenty when I felt like I was just beginning to know her as Sonia Peterson and not just as "mama". I had no idea what my life would become during a time of anguish and grief uncertainty loomed over me, but I knew I had to take life by its wings and hope to soar.

Within a span of six months, life changed completely for my brother, my mom, and me. From October 2012 to April 2013, we faced countless doctor visits, hospital stays, rehabilitation centers, and the emotional roller coaster of my mom's battle with lymphoma cancer. Before this, I had never truly understood the impact of cancer or what it meant to have a loved one go through such a diagnosis.

Allow me to take you back to a crucial memory that shaped my story and the grief I experienced. I was at work one day, ready to take a break and retrieve my cell phone from my locker. As I unlocked my phone, I noticed multiple missed calls, and I immediately knew something was wrong with my mom. My mind spiraled into the worst-case scenario. I called my brother back, and with relief in his voice, he said, "Mom wants to talk to you." The weight on my shoulders lifted, and I eagerly awaited her call. She wanted me to visit her at the hospital that night, even though it was well past visiting hours. Knowing my family's determination, my dad drove me to the hospital after my shift ended.

As I entered the hospital room, family members gathered in the hallways, their worries palpable. I approached my mom, took her hand, and asked how she was doing. She replied, "I'm good." Then, she proceeded to share what the doctors had told her earlier that day, presenting her with two choices that ultimately led to the same outcome. It was a difficult decision, and she wanted my brother and me to be a part of it. I won't delve into the details of that conversation, but I will say that no one should ever have to face such a question in their lifetime.

I vividly remember my mom returning home, confined to a hospital bed with a breathing machine and her nurse by her side. At the time, I didn't realize she was on hospice care, nor did I fully understand what hospice entailed. The hospice company provided my brother and me with a book, which outlined the days leading up to the individual's death while under hospice care. It described the signs to look for, the requests they might make, the changes in their physical and mental state, and more.

One passage mentioned the individual's skin turning blue. So, every day, I would examine my mom's feet, searching for that hint of blue. When I didn't see it, a glimmer of hope ignited within me, believing that God had a plan to heal her, despite the doctors' prognosis. Even having that book, my heart held onto the belief that healing was possible and God had a ram in the bush.

Then came April 26, 2013. I visited my mom at home that morning before heading to work. Holding her hand, I whispered, "If you can hear me, squeeze my hand." And she did. A smile spread across my face. I lay next to her on the bed, watching TV, before preparing to leave. Once again, I reached for her hand, gave it a gentle squeeze, and kissed her cheek. "Okay, Mama, I'll see you later. I'll come by after work tonight," I said. She nodded, her understanding evident despite the pain she endured. Within an hour of leaving, I received the phone call. Not much was said, but I knew and felt that my mother was no longer here with us.

Losing my mother has been the most traumatic experience of my life so far. Your mother is truly your first best friend. She's there for all your firsts - the first steps, the first words, helping you navigate through puberty and even asking embarrassing questions about crushes. I remember my mom being that embarrassing mother, always showing up at school asking about the guy I liked and calling out his name. I would be mortified and tell her to stop.

But looking back, I appreciate her unwavering support. She was front and center at my school plays, and my brother's basketball and football games, always there cheering us on and supporting our passions. I can't fathom how she managed to work so hard and still show up for us in our extracurricular activities. Now that I'm older, I am incredibly grateful for all the sacrifices she made.

Yet, there's one particular memory that stands out. We didn't have transportation at the time, but we needed to go shopping for school supplies. It was late, and the mall was about to close. My mom had bags in her hands, my brother had bags too, and I was carrying two boxes of shoes on my head. We were running to catch the next metro bus, tired and out of breath. I wanted to give up, but my mom urged me to keep going, saying, "Just keep running, we can make it!" And we did. We made it to the bus, laughing and catching our breath. Moments like these remind me of my mom's determination and perseverance.

In middle school, I decided to join the band and play the trombone. My mom was incredibly supportive, even though deep down, she probably knew it wasn't my forte. Eventually, I realized it wasn't for me and wanted to quit. But my mom insisted that I finish the year before deciding. As an adult, I appreciate her persistence. Whenever I find myself in a difficult situation or wanting to quit, I hear her voice in my head, telling me to finish what I started. I'm grateful that my mom never let us give up and instilled in us the values of commitment and perseverance.

She showed us true strength and determination. My mom exemplified integrity and taught us the importance of being true to our word. She taught us the value of hard work and encouraged us to never give up. Just before she passed away, I started a significant job, but an older lady at work made it incredibly challenging for me. I came home, frustrated, and told my mom that I wanted to quit because it was too much to handle. But she looked at me and said, "You're not going to quit. Don't let someone else make you give up."

That was 11 years ago, and I'm still at the same job. Whenever I face tough situations at work, I hear my mom's voice reminding me not to let anyone make me quit. She knew the importance of that job and believed it would carry me even after she was gone. I am forever grateful for her words, her strength, and her wisdom. The question of how to navigate through grief is one that many struggle with.

There is no one-size-fits-all answer, but I believe there is one essential way to find acceptance and seek peace, and that is through God. Grief doesn't simply disappear; it becomes more manageable over time. You find yourself smiling a little more, crying a little less, and able to share your story without breaking down. But to reach that point, you must seek God for His strength, His peace, His comfort, and His love. He is the only one who can truly carry you through the depths of grief.

Finding healing and processing grief requires intentionality. In this life, we will face various challenges, and it's crucial to confront them before they consume us. These challenges can range from grief and heartache to spiritual warfare, depression, anxiety, and more. Grief is not solely about losing a loved one; it's about coming to terms with the absence of something you once had. Through it all, remember who you are and whose you are. Have unwavering faith in your purpose and seek God daily, knowing that He will never fail you.

Losing a loved one, especially a parent, is incredibly difficult. But when I reflect on who I am today, I am grateful to God. I thank Him for not allowing me to succumb to grief and weakness. Instead, He has transformed my pain into purpose. I never thought I would make it through. Hope seemed impossible to hold onto. The words echoed in my mind, sung by the legendary Whitney Houston in her song "I Didn't Know My Own Strength", I am forever grateful that my mother has found peace in heaven's gates, and I am thankful for the constant presence of my forever guardian angel watching over me and my family.

To The Readers

Living with grief is a complex and deeply personal journey that is unique to everyone. It is a process that encompasses a wide range of emotions, experiences, and challenges as one navigates through the pain and loss that accompanies grief. While grief can be overwhelming and seemingly insurmountable, it is possible to find ways to live with grief and gradually find healing and meaning amidst the sorrow.

One of the first things to acknowledge when living with grief is that it is a natural and necessary response to loss. Grief is not something to be avoided or suppressed but rather a reflection of the love and connection that existed between us and the person or thing we have lost. It is a testament to the depth of our emotions and the impact that loss has on our lives.

Living with grief involves allowing ourselves to experience and express our emotions fully. It is essential to create space for sadness, anger, confusion, and any other emotions that may arise. Suppressing or denying these emotions can prolong the healing process and hinder our ability to move forward. By acknowledging and accepting our feelings, we can begin to process them and find healthier ways to cope.

It is also important to understand that grief is not linear. It does not follow a predictable timeline or set of stages. It is a fluid and ever-changing experience that can ebb and flow over time. Some days may feel easier, while others may be filled with intense pain. It is crucial to be patient and compassionate with ourselves as we navigate these fluctuations, allowing ourselves to grieve in our own unique way and at our own pace.

Living with grief often involves finding support from others. Connecting with loved ones, friends, or support groups who have also experienced loss can provide a sense of understanding and validation. Sharing our stories, fears, and struggles with others who have walked a similar path can be incredibly comforting and can help us feel less alone in our grief. Professional support, such as therapy or counseling, can also be beneficial in navigating the complexities of grief and finding healthy coping mechanisms.

Amid grief, hold onto your faith, seek God's strength, and allow Him to guide you through the healing process. Remember that even in the darkest moments, there is hope for a brighter tomorrow.

You're absolutely right! The pain we experience in life can serve as a catalyst to propel us towards our purpose. The challenges and trials we face are not meant to break us, but to push us towards the place that God has prepared for us.

In Jeremiah 29:11, it is written, "For I know the plans I have for you," declares the LORD, "plans to prosper you and not to harm you, plans to give you hope and a future." This verse reminds us that God has a specific plan and purpose for each of us, and it includes peace, well-being, and a hopeful future.

Trusting the process can be difficult, especially when we are faced with pain and uncertainty. But we must hold onto our faith and believe that in the end, when it's all said and done, everything works out just the way God intended. Have confidence in God that he is working behind the scenes, orchestrating events for our benefit.

So, during pain and challenges, hold onto your faith, trust in God's plan, and know that He is leading you toward your purpose. Allow your pain to push you towards the place God has prepared for you and remember that everything works out for the good of those who believe.

To Our Mom

Mom, you taught us the true meaning of love, selflessness, and strength. Your unconditional love and unwavering support were the foundation of our lives. We cherish every moment spent together, every smile shared, and every tear wiped away.

You were our guiding light, our pillar of strength, and our source of inspiration. You pushed us to reach for the stars and never settle for less than our dreams. Your determination and perseverance taught us to never give up, no matter the obstacles we face.

Your love extended beyond our family, as you touched the lives of everyone you met. Your kindness, compassion, and warmth made a lasting impact on all who had the privilege of knowing you. You had a way of making others feel seen, heard, and valued.

As we reflect on the memories we created, we are filled with gratitude for the time we had together. From family vacations to quiet moments at home, each memory holds a special place in our hearts. We will forever cherish the laughter, the conversations, and the love that filled our home.

Though we wish we could have had more time with you, we find solace in knowing that your love will forever guide us. Your spirit lives on in the lessons you taught us and the values you instilled in us. We carry your legacy with us, striving to make you proud with every step we take.

Mom, thank you for being an incredible woman. Your love, strength, and unwavering presence will

forever be cherished. We are blessed to have had you as our mother, and we will continue to honor your memory in everything we do.
Love,

Kim & Tim

In Loving Memory

Sonia Peterson

Sunrise September 21, 1974
Sunset April 26, 2013

Trust in the Lord *with all your heart and lean not on your own understanding; in all your ways submit to him, and he will make your paths straight.*
Proverbs 3:5-6

Ashley Arrington

"From Grief to Grace"

For His "GRACE" is sufficient! I have never experienced a loss that did not end with insurmountable feelings of pain, hurt, and numbness. Yet life has shown me that these moments afforded me more grace and helped to cultivate my relationship with God. In November 2016, God spoke to me and told me to prepare for my mother's death. I heard God loud and clear, but I wanted to ignore the instructions for the sake of holding on to my mother for as long as I could.

During this season of my life, I was blinded by the enemy's agenda, and boy did he think he was winning–but God!!! "Queen", is the nickname that I called my mother. Queen would always tell me not to worry about her because God had her. I knew our God had her and now has her, but the thought of losing her was too much to bear.

In November 2016, a new thing happened. A new relationship was developing with a young woman who told me," I'm not going to be any good for you." I took that as a challenge, and I challenged it because I was overwhelmed with lust and infatuation for this young lady.

Queen did not agree with my lifestyle, but instead of disowning me, she chose to love me. I cherished my Queen with my whole heart because she chose to allow God to work in my life, versus her trying to dictate and control my life.

In January 2017, I received a call from my TT, Fonda stating that my Queen was in the hospital and the doctors had given up and they had done all they could do. I recalled the day when God spoke, yet I didn't pay any mind to what He said. It wasn't until I called my mom's husband 'June Bug' to confirm what I had been told that it began to sink in. He confirmed it and I immediately called my dad to ask him what I should do while being stressed.

He said, "Ashley, that is your momma, come on home!" At the time, I had been living in Houston for almost three years and my queen was back home in Jackson, MS. So, I drove to Jackson, with the sole intention of only going to check on my mom in the hospital. When I arrived in Jackson, I greeted my family and raced to my queen's hospital room.

I approached the door of her hospital room with the biggest smile on my face. I yelled, "Heyyy Queen!"

She looked at me with the biggest smile, and said, "Hey, my BAPS!"

Turns out she had double pneumonia in both lungs along with other ailments such as uncontrolled diabetes, renal failure, and an unexpected emergency leg amputation.

Suddenly, the hospital transferred her to the ICU because the pneumonia was affecting her breathing. My family gathered around the waiting room and the spirit of sadness was simply overwhelming. I excused myself to locate my queen's nurse to get a better explanation of what was going on with my mom.

Once I located her, she explained all that my queen was experiencing. She put her hand on my shoulder and said, "Baby, your mom is going to be alright", with the biggest smile. From that moment, the atmosphere was set for me to praise God anyhow. I stood there anticipating the next visiting hour for the ICU. While waiting for the next time, I looked over at my family and told them that the nurse said my momma would be okay. Even though they chose to sit in sadness, I was encouraged to meet them with joy.

God had given me peace amid the storm. I urged them to lean on God. The next visiting hour came, and

I remembered God instructing me to lay hands on my mother and pray over her. So, I did what I was instructed to do. As she was incubated with tubes running all around her, I grabbed her hand and began to pray. I declared, "God said you shall live and not die!" I repeated it three times. At that moment, I decided not to leave Jackson until I saw my mom in a better state of health.

As I stood there, instantly, her eyes popped open. What I experienced next was supernatural. I was so overwhelmed with joy! I ran out to my family to share what had happened and they couldn't believe it. As each day passed, she progressed and before we knew it, she was back to herself, smiling and ready to eat! She was later transferred to a nursing home to receive rehab.

As months progressed, she progressed. Life was great and looking favorable until the relationship with the young lady I was dating started to fail. I called my mom to tell her everything that was going on. While she normally said something or gave her advice, this day, she sat quietly on the phone and listened to me vent. I received a call from a close cousin so, I told my mom that I would call her back.

Little did I know that clicking over to take another call would result in never hearing my queen's voice again. The very next morning, I was awakened by a phone call from my brother saying, "Ash, mama is gone!" I instantly hung up the phone and dialed her number. I waited for her to answer, but there was no answer. I laid back in the bed and stared at the ceiling fan. All I could think about was not calling my momma back and that I would never get to talk to her again. That was a pain I had never experienced before.

I had lost loved ones, but to hear of my mama the woman who carried me in her womb and throughout my life is dead, was hard to phantom. This time around grief was different for me. I wasn't given the proper opportunity to grieve due to the distractions of mental and emotional abuse that caused the overshadowing of grieving the reality of my queen no longer with me.

I remember so vividly, the day we laid my queen to rest, I was bombarded with phone calls by the estranged person at the time who had a heavy influence in my life. Now this may sound crazy, but I thought the bombarded phone calls were her checking up on me. However, it was her selfish character asking me for money to fund her addiction.

I want to take this opportunity to highlight the details of this relationship. At the beginning of the relationship, I just wanted to be happy and to be loved by someone. I felt like she provided this, but throughout the relationship, I began to learn that no one can love me like God. His love didn't come with conditions.

This new relationship almost cost me my life. The woman ended up being a manipulative drug addict, a narcissist, and very abusive. I had already been through a lot in my life, so this became another challenge I had to overcome. I went through some of the worst times I had ever experienced in my life.

The relationship became violent and unsafe for both of us. Throughout that whole year of dating this woman, I never knew she was pregnant. It was not until I received a phone call informing me to rush to The Women's Hospital because a baby girl was about to be born. Now this may sound crazy, but little did I know I would become a bonus mother to a baby girl by the name of Nova Jewel Arrington. Ironically, she was born one day before my birthday.

I wasn't prepared to raise a child. For God's sake, I was still trying to process my mother's passing while being emotionally and mentally abused throughout this relationship. God has a funny way of showing up and providing solutions at the most critical times. This beautiful bundle of joy created a sense of peace and calmness as my mother would have.

There would be days when I would sit and think about the relationship and bond that my queen and I shared, and I would become sad. In those moments, the baby would sound off for my attention. She became my shadow.

In October 2017, I heard God's voice so clearly when he asked me to seek Him. I was confused about how and where to start to accomplish this request. One thing I knew was to pray, when I began to pray, I spoke to God so honestly and said, "God I need to give my life back over to you and I'd do whatever you need of me just please deliver me from this toxic relationship".

It was not until one Sunday when an argument that typically happened turned into a physical fight. I was held hostage in my apartment for three hours with a knife pointed at my throat. I finessed my way to get outside of my apartment by telling her that I would drop her and the child off at her mother's. She quickly went and sat outside while holding the baby who only had a diaper on. I ran past her and down the stairs to hop into my truck. She followed me and started stabbing at my tires while still holding the baby with the same knife she held to my throat. I managed to escape without her, and the baby being hurt.

Amid my despair, God would send His angels to comfort and remind me of His grace. Believe it or not, I questioned God while I was in that relationship, but I knew what my mom instilled in me. His grace proved that I would live and not die.

One month after coming to my senses, God told me He was going to purge me of the old and do a new thing within me. It was time for the new wineskins because the old wineskins had run their course. Whatever was of God and from God, I wanted it!

The year came to an end, and I was instructed to enter into a season of isolation. In that season, it was just me and God. I was instructed to only attend church, work, and back home. I got baptized and rededicated my life back to Christ. He unscaled my eyes and removed the spirit of homosexuality.

God would reveal to me in my time spent with Him, how He protected me even when I doubted Him. I would ask about my mom dying and the baby being born. That's when He told me I wasn't mentally prepared to grieve my queen's passing due to all I had going on. I was at peace when I sat and soaked in His presence. He would show me how He gave me strength during the preparation of the homegoing celebration for my queen along with the day of. Everyone thought I was just distraught and down, but I was at peace. God gave me peace during those times. His grace did not fail me even when I called myself a failure.

Seven years later, His grace is still sufficient! I am thankful for the new beginnings and the fresh start that God has given me. I am no longer held captive by the past, but I am free to embrace the future that God has planned for me. His grace has brought me through every trial and every storm, and I know that His grace will continue to sustain me in the days ahead.

I am forever grateful for His grace that is always sufficient, even in the darkest moments of life. I am thankful for His love that never fails and His mercy that endures forever. I am confident that His grace will continue to be more than enough for me, no matter what challenges may come my way.

Thank you, God, for your amazing grace! Grief looks different to every individual and so I received grace instead of grief. Rosalind (my queen) is forever in my heart, and I know she would be astounded to read this chapter. I thank God daily for using me as his vessel. Grief could not hold me bound.

In Loving Memory

Rosalind Arrington Jones

Sunrise October 19, 1965
Sunset March 16, 2017

I can do all things through Christ that strengthens me. Philippians 4:13,

LaTeshia Bailey

"Daddy's Not So Little Girl"

During the peak of a global pandemic, I was undergoing grief counseling for a different type of loss, when I received a phone call from my cousin saying, "Cousin, I found Uncle Pee Wee. He's at Houston Methodist. You really should come see about your dad, he's not doing good, and I really think you should be here."

Now, imagine saying throughout your life that if something ever happened to him, I won't be there and if he ever passes away, I will not attend the funeral. I was just that angry and convinced my life would go on as if he never existed.

Well, I am convinced you should never say never, because you might have to eat those words. It took me a minute to gather my thoughts and bypass my anger. When I finally chose to visit my father in early May of 2021, I was there non-stop for two weeks serving as the go-to person for someone who was never a constant in my life.

All my life, I longed for the father-daughter bond. I longed to be acknowledged as "daddy's" little girl. Being with him provided a very brief opportunity for me to experience being his daughter, but there would be little to no reciprocation of him being a father because his life on earth ended within two weeks.

I remember going to visit my dad, whom I called Pops, at the hospital after my cousin informed me where he was. I remember walking in the door and saying, "Hey Pops!" and he turned his head to the door and started balling. The kind of cry you give when you're happy to see someone after so long but are sorry for all you put them through, type of cry. I recall wiping his tears as they fell. I said, "Pop's, I'm here for you. I don't want or expect anything from you in return, just let me be here for you."

I kissed him on the forehead and stood next to him glancing at his grey beard, frail body, and hearing his soft faint voice. I couldn't help but notice how my dad had aged. The last time I saw him was seven years prior. It was typical for us to go several years without communication as that was our unhealthy pattern. One of us would eventually make a move to reconnect only to fall out of good terms again after a short period.

Standing there I heard him say, "Baby girl I'm tired. My body is giving out and I'm dying." I told the doctor what he had shared with me, and the doctor said, "Oh no ma'am, he's not dying he has more years ahead of him." Of course, I took the doctor's word over my Pops because it was more positive news than what Pops gave.

A few days later I received a call that my Pops took a turn for the worse. He knew his body and he was right. A few days before he took a turn my big brother and I were in the room with him.

He told us he wanted us to be his medical power of attorney which called for us to make and carry out all of the final decisions in the hospital. How did I get such a huge responsibility bestowed upon me when he was never there for me? How was I to see this through? I was already dealing with so much as a newly single mom. I worked a full-time demanding job that was considered essential during a global pandemic.

Things began moving at a fast pace to the point where my days and nights were running together. I started getting call after call from the medical team attending to my Pops. The more they called the more I questioned how and why I was the one doing all of this. Everything was happening so quickly.

Thankfully around New Year's of 2021, my Pops reached out to me and told me he was ready to listen to me, uninterrupted, about how I felt concerning our relationship. I poured out my heart to him. As the parent, I always expected him to be the bigger person and mend our relationship, but I always felt I had to be the bigger person and make things right.

Our fallout would end in me being cursed out and my feelings getting hurt pretty badly. He missed so many important moments in my life that the hurt and abandonment just continued to build up over the years. He stood me up one Christmas as a young teenager and that is when I shut down from trusting his word. He missed my high school graduation in May 2002 at the age of 18, that his sisters, my cousins, and my brother attended, but not him. He always wanted to take part in my accomplishments, and I didn't think it was fair because he never supported me and was never there when I wanted him to be.

The crazy thing is we desired a relationship with each other so badly. A piece of my life was missing. It was like standing in front of a two-way mirror where we could see each other but not see each other at the same time. We were looking and seeing a reflection of ourselves because we were both being stubborn.

We mended things around 2014 when I was getting married and fell out right before the wedding because he wanted to walk me down the aisle and I wouldn't let him. My stepdad had been a constant in my life since I was ten and that was his honor to bestow. The next year I gave birth to my son, and he tried to make things right. He bought my son so many clothes, shoes, toys, blankets, etc. for Christmas of 2015.

My cousin, my brother, and my son's dad told me I should call to say thank you. I did just that. He missed my first call and tried calling back, but his number was blocked from our last fallout. I unblocked him and received his call. He told me he wanted to see his grandson and I told him before he could we needed to talk about how he cursed me out before my wedding. He became furious and cursed me out.

From that moment on we went right back to having no communication for six years. He did not see or talk to my son until his deathbed. He was the last person my Pops laid eyes on via video chat before his eternal rest. That was the first and last time he saw my son. Before he took a turn for the worst, he gave my cousin sixty dollars to give me and told me he wanted me to buy my son a red remote-control car. I found the biggest one I could and gifted it to my son. My son still has that car to this very day.

I can recall the day my older brother walked into the hospital room and said, "There is a God, LaTeshia Marie is feeding James Donald. I never thought I'd see the day." To be honest I never thought I would see it either, but God has a funny way of making us do the right thing even when we don't want to.

During the days when his health was deteriorating his nurse gave me a beautiful cross with a heart and Angel wings. She handled my Pops with care. I'll forever be grateful for her. On a certain day, I received a call and headed up to the hospital. Pops was heavily sedated to keep him asleep and with the least amount of discomfort. The nurse asked me if I wanted them to turn the sedation off so I could talk with him and I said yes. This was the day it got surreal.

He had a tube down his throat so he couldn't speak properly. He could mouth words around the tube, but it was so hard to understand. I got the idea to make an alphabet chart and get some paper to write down the words he created with the letters he pointed to.

Eventually, they formed sentences that I was able to understand. He told me he wanted to live and wanted me to pray with him for that. Soon after he told me God was calling him home. He would go into trances during our conversations in which he would see our deceased loved ones. On one occasion it was my Aunt Red he saw standing behind me. I thought the nurse was behind me because I felt a presence but when I turned around no one was there. He asked me where Red went, and I told him she was in Heaven.

During another instance, he saw my grandmother at the foot of his bed, my Aunt Red, my Aunt Cheeta, and my Aunt Stein. One day while at the hospital, he told me it was time to let him go. I asked, "Why me?" and he replied, "Because you are the only one holding on to me." He was absolutely correct because the first time in my life I finally felt like daddy's little girl at 37 years old.

I remember everyone leaving the room and there I was sitting in a chair facing his bed. He pointed to the corner and told me my granny was standing there. I asked him if she could see me, and he said, "Yes, and that she loves me." At that moment I knew it was time to grant him the release that he requested, and I broke.

With a loud voice, as I sobbed, I cried out "DADDY!!!" Something I never called him directly before. My family in the hall heard my cry as well as the staff on duty. I fell to my knees on the floor and cried out, "Why Daddy, why now, don't leave me!"

Everything was finally right but maybe God wanted it that way. The air was clear between us. We were getting along. We had bonding time and shared some real heart-to-heart moments. How do you let go when things are finally how you desired them to be all your life? I had no choice.

A couple of days after he passed away, I was in a store when I got a phone call to go outside right away. The person on the phone was so excited I had to go and see what all the excitement was about. I went outside to witness the most beautiful double rainbow that draped the sky. It stopped everyone in their tracks.

People everywhere were taking photos and videos in awe of its splendor. Seeing that gave me the peace I was longing for since Pops went on to glory. It made my spirit happy that I had prayed the Lord's Prayer with Pops and that he asked for forgiveness of all his known and unknown sins. I felt he made it to our Heavenly Father.

In the days after his passing, I'd done things I'd never done before like preparing for his funeral, picking out clothes with my siblings, and helping create an obituary. Going through old photos caused so many memories to rush through my mind. The day came to lay him to rest. He was so handsome and looked so youthful. I still wasn't ready to let go.

As mentioned before I was already in grief counseling and had to incorporate this part into my counseling sessions. How do I move forward from here? I craved the connection that was created during those final two weeks of his life. So many questions filled my heart and mind as to why we could not accomplish what was done in two weeks in the 37 years I had him here. Why did he have to die now? There should've been more time. Tomorrow is not promised to any of us.

Things may not go the way you plan but if you have someone here on earth that you have strife with, don't wait until tomorrow to pick up the phone or make a visit and try to reconcile your differences. When they are gone it'll always be what if and those what ifs will go unanswered. Enroll in grief counseling if you have already lost your loved one. Reminisce on the good moments you shared with them. Get a journal and write about them, look at old photos that will highlight good memories.

When you're down find someone who will listen to you. Get a friend or family member who can help you elaborate on the good times. Grieving is a process that tends to get a little easier with time but never really goes away. Do something to keep their memory alive or do something in their honor that will put a smile on your face to bring you joy even in their absence. Don't put off what can be done today for tomorrow.

In Loving Memory

James Donald Scott

AKA: Hacksaw, PeeWee, Big Daddy

Sunrise March 10, 1966
Sunset May 17, 2021

And we know that all things work together for good to them that love God, to them who are the called according to his purpose. Romans 8:28 KJV

Simone Gooden

"Grieving Gracefully"
A Short Memoir in Honor of Troy Gooden, Sr.

The adolescent effect that parenting has on children is critical to the overall development of who they will become in adulthood. Your parents are your very first earthly image and example of life and leadership. Growing up early on it was evident that I was my mother's twin and a daddy's girl at heart. Since birth, my dad's presence had been felt and appreciated. I had the kind of father that did it all.

He was the protector of the home, the breadwinner financially, a devoted husband, and a real father in every sense of the word. Family has always been important to me. From grade school programs, band practice, basketball games, and church events to college dorm move-in day, I saw my parents be so supportive and never miss a beat. I could only imagine that support in my adulthood.

I have adopted many traits from my dad, including my outgoing personality, sense of humor, low tolerance for foolishness, and meticulous work ethic. You know what they say. The first daughter is the female version of their daddy. This is so true; I can attest to it. LOL.

It was the first month of the year 2016 when the Lord called my Daddy home. I was only 23 years old and my life as I knew it would be forever changed! I was just a few months away from graduating college, and I was glad to be nearing completion. I remember praying that God would let my Daddy hold on to see me reach this accomplishment. He had been with me through everything, he could not miss this.

The year 2015 had been rough, as my dad was suddenly diagnosed with cancer. The initial diagnosis took me aback. I remember being lost for words. As a young adult, it is hard to see your superhero incapacitated. As he always did, he pushed through and fought hard until his last breath. He passed peacefully around family and loved ones. In his last days, I came to peace with the totality of the disease and its effect on his body. I hated seeing him in pain. His mission here on earth was accomplished!

Looking back, it was selfish for me to want him here. I just was not mentally prepared to see him go. I crossed the stage on graduation day with the loving support of my family. While I didn't have the physical presence of my dad, I overwhelmingly felt his spiritual presence there and knew he was with me every step of the way. It made it even all the better that my aunt, his sister, made it to the graduation to show her support. That meant the world to me.

Grief is so peculiar! It comes and goes, and at times it randomly stops you right in your tracks. Sometimes the slightest and simplest things can remind you of your loved one(s) who have transitioned. Simple things such as hearing Kem play on the radio and seeing boats or 18-wheelers travel down I-45 remind me of my dad. I often reminisce on my childhood fishing trips and family vacations. There are so many fond memories that I hold dear to me.

Shortly after my father's passing, I noticed that red cardinals crossed my path often. They would appear while I was at the park or randomly outside in the sunshine. The first few times this occurred, I thought, "Oh wow, that's interesting." I began to see them more often and researched for context. I discovered that cardinals may be perceived as a peaceful message from a deceased loved one, symbolizing hope and comfort in times of distress.

I often wondered if I was making my dad proud and I would ponder on what his advice would be to me at this point in my life. He provided great advice and always offered so much wisdom, a true teacher. Not only did he give sound advice, but he led by example. I respected this so much. I feel his words of encouragement to my siblings, and I would simply be, "You are doing good, keep going." Something short and sweet; as his mantra was "Your actions and work ethic show everything."

My father's death showed me firsthand that life is short so live it in abundance and to the fullest. Take calculated risks, bet on yourself, and always put God first! You do these things, and you will be remembered long after you have passed on. My father was wise beyond his years, and I can say with confidence that he lived his life to the absolute fullest, coincidentally with him meeting his first grandchild and namesake shortly before his passing. Such a bittersweet moment.

When I think of the word to describe the impact my Daddy had on my life, the word that comes to mind is blessed. I was blessed to have such a loving earthly father. Blessed to grow up in a two-parent household and see two individuals work together in unison with love and dedication. Blessed to be raised by an active father. Blessed to be brought up with faith-based principles and morals. Blessed to have acquired so many gems of knowledge throughout my life from him. Blessed to have the standard and tone set of how a man should treat a woman. I was truly blessed to call him my dad!

Moreover, grief comes in many forms and affects everyone differently. Not only may grief come from the loss of a person but it can also be exemplified through the loss of a relationship. Three years after the death of my father, my marriage had ended. As many young couples, we dealt with the joys and pains of growing up together and navigating life simultaneously.

In the relationship, I can truly say that we saw each other in every season. Happy, sad, mad, broke, paid, and in seasons of grief. He was a great support for me throughout the illness and subsequent death of my father, as I was for him during the illness and death of his stepfather. In these two passings, we clung to one another, providing strength and encouragement to continue on and for that, I am forever grateful.

Toward the end of the marriage, another death occurred. This was a sudden and unexpected loss in his life that 'shook the table' if you will. He lost a close family member, and this loss hit a bit differently. It made him see the world differently and ultimately changed his view on many aspects of life in general. Our marriage was affected instantly by this loss. We tried to work through our issues but ultimately separated a year later and shortly after divorced.

The divorce was hard news for family members and friends to hear because we had so much history together, but this was the right decision for both of us as we had grown apart. Marriage is a teamwork collective effort. Both people have to choose to show up every day. As I have gotten older, I see even more so, how paramount a strong, anchored relationship in Christ is.

I spent the following year focusing on myself and truly healing, rebuilding, and getting back to the basics of life. Even now, I am committed to becoming a better me so when the next man comes into my life, I am open and present to receive love. Love is a beautiful thing and a blessing from up above. I thank God for the beautiful memories and lessons of my previous marriage, and I continue to have a positive outlook on matrimony. I know God has my future husband waiting for me.

Keep The Faith
Just as there are stages of death, there are stages of grief that one should try to work their way through.

Prayerfully, work your way to the last stage, which is acceptance. Acceptance doesn't mean invalidation of feelings or forgetting. It doesn't mean being happy all the time and being fully removed from the feeling of reminiscence.

It means being at peace and grateful for the life that was lived. It means choosing to continue to thrive in life and not succumb to the psychological thoughts of depression, doubt, and fear. We must know that it is okay to cry and properly grieve our loved ones that we miss so dearly!

Take the needed time to reflect and be thankful for the time spent and the love felt. Grief is an ongoing process and the love that we have for our loved ones will never cease to end. Know that you are not alone! We all are dealing with some form of loss and are trying our best to navigate through this journey of life.

I thank God for the bond I have with my siblings. Even now into adulthood, our relationship has continued to grow. I love how we authentically relate with one another. Having a solid support system (family, friends, mentors, etc.) and most importantly, a direct and open relationship with God, has proven to be the most resourceful and beneficial tools to have during times of hardship. I thank God for those who love me and have supported me throughout my life.

Having people you trust and can lean on during hard times is so impactful. It makes all the difference in times of heightened grief or very emotional seasons. This includes moments like your loved ones' birthday or the anniversary of their death (especially the first few years). If it had not been for the Lord on my side, I don't know where I would be, literally!

There are other therapeutic measures that include individual therapy and commonality group therapy as coping mechanisms. It is always great to have the support of others who can directly relate to what you are going through. Journaling has also been a great implementation I use to effectively express myself. I aim to do a morning devotion to start my day with the love of God.

Moreover, I know it may sound cliché but give yourself and others grace! Every day will not be a good day and that is ok! Embrace the good with the bad. On good days, be grateful. On bad days, be grateful also.

Lastly, work, grind, and hustle HARD! Faith without work is dead. Prayer without application is void. Stay focused on things that have a purpose in your life and that push you forward. Keep going and keep growing. Work hard at your personal goals and aspirations. There is no time for idleness.

Won't He Do It–Restoration

Fast forward to today, God has blessed and restored me in ways I could not have imagined! I am overall in a better place mentally and spiritually than I have been in years. I am very intentional with who and what I give my time to. I have clarity and reflection from the past and apply thoughtful execution to my future. I am not a victim but a victor in life. Perspective is everything and anything that happens in my life, God permitted it, therefore I can stand it and be able to navigate through it. The mindset in which you see things is pivotal to how you will maneuver forward. It dictates your trajectory!

God blessed me to be able to execute something I put off for many years, which was to go back to school. I was accepted into my desired program and completed my graduate degree in one year. I have a great career that I thoroughly enjoy. I have been able to foster and cultivate relationships with friends and family. Most of all, I'm thankful for joy and peace that surpasses all understanding! These intangible and priceless things mean the most to me. I am grateful for them. I thank God for a spirit of resoluteness. His mercies are new every morning!

When it comes to uncontrolled circumstances, I have a "It is what it is" mindset. No need to worry over things that are out of my control because I know God will provide, as He always has. He is a restorer, and we must know that all things work out for the good of those who love God. The best is yet to come!

Prayer of Praise & Thanksgiving

Dear Lord, thank you for one more opportunity to give you praise. Thank you for this book of collections from resilient black women and our experiences with grief. May our stories help or encourage someone. Thank you for our loved ones who are no longer here with us. Thank you for relationships that have ended and new ones that have begun. Thank you for the good times, the lessons, the blessings, the words of wisdom, and the beautiful memories shared! May these memories stay near and dear to our hearts as we continue their legacy. Lastly, Heavenly Father, I thank you for the gift of eternal life. For we know that if we believe in your son Jesus Christ, we will one day reunite with our loved ones. Keep us, comfort us, and have us continue to walk in our earthly purpose. In your holy name, I do pray. Amen.

May my short words of resolution provide all reading this book comfort and peace during times of grief. God bless!

In Loving Memory

Troy D. Gooden Sr.

Sunrise July 18, 1962
Sunset January 19, 2016

I have fought the good fight, I have finished the race, I have kept the faith. Now there is in store for me the crown of righteousness, which the Lord, the righteous Judge, will award to me on that day—and not only to me, but also to all who have longed for his appearing. 2 Timothy 4:7-8

Natarsha Hackney

"Until The Last Breath"

Have you ever wondered why bad things happen to good people? Why does it appear that no matter how much you invest in living right, trouble tends to locate you at the oddest times and in the hardest ways? These were only a few of the questions I pondered during the untimely death of my grandparents. Two people who meant the world to me lost their lives in a very tragic manner.

I was born in the home with my grandparents, but at some point, my mother moved out and took me with her. During my high school years, I went back to live with them. At first, I was the only child in the home, but eventually, my brothers came to live with us. I was very close to them, and I can honestly say they were old school and did not play. I loved them both so much.

As time progressed my grannie was diagnosed with dementia, but my grandfather who was aging as well was doing okay. In February 2021, Texas was hit with a winter freeze that caused major damages and deaths in various parts of the United States. When I heard about the storm, I was immediately concerned about my grandparents being alone without anyone to care for them. We had no idea how impactful this storm would be, but when it made landfall there were many without lights and ways to keep warm. I still had lights in my home, so I called around and told a couple of family members that I could pick up my grandparents and bring them to my house.

Let me interject a few words of wisdom. When you have an urge or gut feeling to do something don't question it because having to deal with regret can be paralyzing.

The thought of picking up my grandparents would not leave me, but I thought they would be okay until I was able to get to them. Little did I know that I would receive a call from my cousin telling me my grandparents' home was on fire. Hearing those words caused me to go numb.

When I realized what was said, I started hyperventilating and having a panic attack. I grabbed my things and ran to the car, but I was scared to drive based on the condition of the roads being reported on the news. The drive to my grandparent's home felt as if I was walking to the death chamber after being sentenced to death in prison. The closer I got the harder my heartbeat. The house was so inflamed I could see the smoke from afar.

I started calling people before I made it to the house. When I pulled up the site was devastating. I could not believe my childhood home was gone and to a fire of all things. The thought of this happening when I considered going to get them was bizarre. The fire was so bad the local news was on-site reporting the damage and the passing of my elderly grandparents.

Once they were located in the home, they were rushed to Lyndon B. Johnson Hospital. The family rushed to the hospital in anticipation that there may be some hope. But my brother was convinced that they were gone based on how they both looked. We sat for over two hours waiting for someone to come and tell us something, anything.

Someone from the medical team finally informed us that my grandparents were no longer with us. My body went limp, but I had to see them one last time. I walked to the room where they both lay looking so peaceful and at rest. At that moment I couldn't help but thank God that they didn't suffer in the fire. According to the firefighters, it appeared that my grandfather took my grandmother to the back room to protect her. They were both trapped in this burning house because the burglar bars secured the windows, and they could not make it to the front door.

At that moment I tried not to think about the fear or torment they both experienced. I chose to focus on the fact that they were both together until their last breath. One did not have to worry about going through life alone without the other and though it was a tragic ending, their union began in love and ended in love.

The family was distraught. I have to admit I was angry for several reasons. For one I should have gone with my first mind and picked them up. Two, the government should have done a better job preparing for the winter storm. There were so many houses catching on fire and innocent lives being lost.

Our family was not prepared for a double funeral, so we created a GoFundMe page to assist with the funeral arrangements because my grandparents were living off retirement. I believe that we should have received some reciprocity from the government because there was another family who experienced the same thing, and they received millions. I worked very hard to get our story out there, but it didn't seem to have the same impact. Many said the family lost their grandparents and their children, but I didn't think it should make a difference. Both sets of individuals lost their lives in a fire during the storm.

Let's fast forward to the funeral. I was already struggling with the loss of two people who had been there for me my entire life when I found out my job denied me time off because they were not my biological parents. It was so bizarre that coworkers were trying to donate their hours and the company would not accept it. I went back to work as expected but I was exhausted and eventually spiraled into a state of depression. I was completely despondent and unable to be present in any space, especially at work.

I started experiencing anxiety to the point where I had to begin seeing a therapist. She placed me on pills to calm my anxiety, but I started abusing the pills to avoid the present reality. I was living each day feeling numb and nonexistent.

On the day of the funeral, I struggled to sit there looking at double caskets. Sitting there looking at the program reading Benjamin Williams Cooks & Virginia Ruth McAdams Cooks was overwhelming, but again beautiful because it was the end of a beautiful love story. A love story I could only hope to experience one day. During this time, I was living with my ex-fiancé who didn't show up the way I needed him to. He shut down at a time when I needed him the most. We didn't bury my grandparents on the same day, but he refused to go to the burial site to support me. This was the straw that broke the camel's back. Going through all of this propelled me into a state of mind that would require me to finally focus on myself.

2021 was a year of awakening for me. I was convinced that like Job from the bible, no matter what I lost, my heavenly Father was going to give it back double for all my trouble. Losing my loved ones opened doors I could have never imagined. Life began to take on new perspectives and I was no longer looking from the same lenses. I found a new appreciation for life and where I once took it for granted, I was now more grateful and patient with self. I learned to drop my unrealistic expectations of others and learned to understand that people would be people, but God would always be God and He never failed.

I found peace amid the storms. I started eating right and losing weight. For the first time in my life, I started living and the light I was created to live in and shine for others had finally manifested. I hate that it took such a significant loss to finally start winning, but

I know my grandparents are smiling down on me. I know they are with me daily and that I draw from their strength and the love they showed our family.

Therefore, I encourage anyone who is in a state of grief to be patient with self. Allow yourself to feel because you are human and losing a loved one can create real pain that can lead to destructive behavior. Learn to focus on the positive aspects of the loss and not the negative, because we have no control over the length of time someone has in our lives. Yes, we want people to live forever, but this is not realistic because we are all scheduled to leave this life one day.

But until that time comes, live your life to the FULLEST!! Do not let the cares of this world stop you from receiving God's best for your life. Do your best to fulfill your purpose by making every moment count "Until you take your last breath!"

In Loving Memory

Benjamin Williams & Virginia Ruth Cooks III

Sunrise 8/20/1950
Sunset 2/15/2021

Sunrise 6/1/1950
Sunset 2/15/2021

So, they are no longer two, but one flesh. Therefore, what God has joined together, let no one separate.
Matthew 19:6

Lisa Johnson

"Death By Suicide"

Death is imminent! There is no avoiding it or prolonging the inevitable, especially for those who have lived a full life and accomplished all they were created to do. But what happens when death comes before its time? What happens when the pressure of life drives an individual to the point of no return? I have pondered this question for quite some time.

I have had to piece together scattered thoughts surrounding the idea of how suicide becomes the solution to tackle life's difficulties. I have had to settle with the fact that some people are not as mentally and emotionally strong as others. Therefore, I do not have the right to assume that someone could or should make a better choice for his or her life.

Reaching this conclusion was not easy, but one I had to settle into when I lost my sweet baby boy to suicide at the tender age of nineteen on April 17, 2011. I was twenty-one years old when I gave birth to Jameel Woods on April 27, 1992. Unfortunately, his father was in prison during the birth and the early years of Jameel's life. His father was released from prison when he was ten. I was enrolled in nursing school which called for me to relocate and Jameel decided to live with my mother because he wanted to stay and play football in his hometown.

Upon the release of his father, Jameel was able to spend some quality time with his father, but just after a year of being released, Jameel's father suffered a heart attack while driving home from work and passed away. Little did we know that tragedy would strike in his life again at the tender age of sixteen when my mother passed away. She practically raised him therefore this was not going to be an easy loss. My daughter and I moved back to Bay City, Texas, my hometown, to care for my son after the loss of my mom.

My son was a senior in high school who played sports and was well-liked and known by many. He had a promising future ahead of him, but he was overcome by a spirit of depression. The classic cliché, "When it rains, it pours" is an understatement.

Not only did he lose his father, his uncle/mentor James and grandmother, but his best friend/girlfriend of seven years broke up with him. Jameel was very excited about attending the University of Texas, but after finding out he had applied too late, he had to attend the University of Houston, in which he was not happy about at all.

Jameel moved to Houston with his grandmother, on his father's side. One day she called and said, "Lisa I don't know what is happening with Jameel, but he has been riding the exercise bike nonstop all night and I feel that something is not right with him." She asked if I would pick him up. I jumped into mommy mode and went to get my baby. When he got in the car, I asked him what was going on. He said he was feeling depressed and hearing voices. He admitted that he needed help. There are no words to describe how I felt in that moment.

Even though he opted to live with my mother, it never stopped me from being a mother. I carried Jameel for nine months; therefore, our connection could never be broken. There would never be a time I could not feel his hurt or know that he was struggling. My job as his mother was to grant his request and get him some help. The following day I took him to see a psychologist.

He did well for the first month. They admitted him into an adult hospital in Houston, but for some reason, there was little to no progress. Then he expressed how he would like to work on a farm with animals. So, I reached out to a friend in another state that owned a facility with horses, which he loved, and was there for three months. Then the rain started pouring again! The facility lost funding and he had to return home. This created an epic decline.

Jameel started talking about different ways to die. He asked me if I thought people would attend his funeral and if I would miss him. As a mother I heard him, but I did not HEAR him!! I thought he was simply being inquisitive like most teenagers. But this talk of death took a drastic turn when he started watching videos about ways to kill yourself. I was in TOTAL denial! My son would never hurt himself. We had a great relationship. He was an awesome star football player with great friends and a community who loved him and that contagious smile. Jameel had a very promising future. Where was this coming from?

Watching my son spiral out of control and hit a social decline was extremely hard for me. I could not sleep because I was afraid to leave him alone. He would jump in his sleep and ask if I heard the voices. The voices? Now I was getting freaked out. So, I had to quit my job to take care of him because I was on constant suicide watch.

I can recall my nephew coming by on prom night and Jameel gave him his watch, as if to give him something to remember him by. On April 16, 2011, he called and asked me to bring him some BBQ. I got the BBQ and went home. This particular night I should have been up all night to watch Jameel, but after not sleeping for two nights straight, I fell asleep and woke up to the daylight shining on my face.

Ironically, myself, my daughter, and Jameel, were set to attend "Family and Friends Day" at church that Sunday morning. As usual, I woke up and posted a spiritual scripture on Facebook, but about "DEATH", which is a subject I never post on. I cannot say if God was preparing me or giving me peace about what was to come.

As soon as I pushed the post button, the neighbor behind us rang the doorbell. I opened the door, and he asked me where Jameel was. I went to his room and saw his phone and wallet on the dresser. The neighbor asked me to follow him to the backyard and that is when my entire life shattered.

There before my very eyes were my son's feet dangling in the air. I could not catch my breath. My head started spinning as it felt like everything around me stopped. I was numb and despondent, but I had to face the hard reality that his thoughts were no longer words, he acted, and his actions resulted in his death.

Once I snapped back into reality, I walked around the tree and saw that he removed the shoestrings from his tennis and hung himself. None of this made any sense. He was always smiling and never appeared to think that anything was wrong. Apparently, there was an internal battle going on. One that not even his mother would comprehend or understand. It was at this moment I let out this blood curling scream from the depth of my soul so loud that my friend living in the apartment complex two blocks away from my home, was awaken out of her sleep and ran barefoot to my home in her pajamas.

As I sat in the passenger seat of my cousin's truck praying continually, I asked God to please send me a sign that I am going to make it through this horrific test of faith. It was within that moment I glanced in the rearview mirror and noticed my pastor as well as two other guest pastors who attended Family and Friends Day at our church.

As they walked down the middle of the street, I could see a silhouette of this huge angel, and a bright light gleaming behind them as they moved in slow motion. I immediately threw my hands up in the air and started saying, "Thank you Jesus over and over again." That was my sign from God that I was going to be alright and to always keep my faith strong in the Lord.

I tried to figure out what could have possibly led to this, but every secret or unmet desire or truth would die with him that dreadful day. It is safe to say that we should NEVER judge a book by its cover because the content may just surprise you. I cried every day for a year. I couldn't eat or sleep which led to a rapid decline in my weight. I went from 265 pounds to 151 pounds in three months.

I definitely could not live in my mom's house any longer. The constant reminder of his tragic death was causing me to come unglued at the seams. I moved and my son's job, HEB, was generous enough to pay my rent up for a year. Grief is tricky and you never know what stage of grief will hit you at any time. Some days I was good, and others were not so good. I was doing the best I could with what I had to work with.

My daughter was nine years old at the time and I remember passing out on the bathroom floor. I could hear her praying for God to save me and that is when I snapped. I had to remember it was not my fault and that I still had another child to live for. I had to remember I am a child of God and He does not allow tests and trials without a TESTIMONY. Now do not get me wrong this was the hardest testimony to gain of my life. But there was a purpose in this loss.

Jameel's life was not in vain. My goal was and is to bring glory to God through his story. I am grateful for the time God allowed me to steward His son because he belonged to God before he was ever given to me. I had to come to terms with the fact that God gives, but He also takes away and there is no questioning what He does or why. I miss my son's electric smile and his charismatic behavior, but I would rather him be at peace than suffer in silence in a world that only adds increased pressure.

Today I am an advocate for suicide. I began breathing life into people who battle with suicidal tendencies. On the surface people who battle with suicide feel lifeless and empty with little to no hope. This is a trick of the enemy, and it is my job to put the enemy on blast and save those who do not have the power to save themselves. There is a silver lining at the end of the rainbow and every time I speak Jameel's story, it brings hope and restoration to the lives of many.

Grief is a process that can be conquered. It may appear that it will never end, but I am a living witness that VICTORY is on the other side waiting to greet you. If you are anyone you know is battling with suicide, please get help. Do NOT suffer in silence. Life is worth living and trouble does not last always. I would like to share the following key points about dealing with suicide:

The signs of suicidal thoughts...

1. Asking if any would come to their funeral
2. Lack of sleep or too much sleep
3. Uneasy, jittery, and low attention span
4. Feeling like a burden to everyone, worthless, and no will to live
5. Severe depression and untimely mood swings
6. Searching for ways to die
7. Blaming themselves for everything

How to help yourself get through suffering the suicidal loss of a loved one...

1. Create a healing space in your home with a chair made from your loved ones' clothing to sit in and look

through pictures.
2. Create a memory book with pictures, scriptures, spiritual encouragements, and poems.
3. Have a bench made at your loved ones' burial site, so you can sit and visit.
4. Have a balloon release on their birthdays; invite family and friends.
5. Start a meaningful project or an organization in their honor.
6. Use one of their shirts as a pillowcase.
7. Have shirts made in their image to wear as needed or to awareness organizations, speech events, and/or representation events.

In Loving Memory

Jameel LaScott Woods

Sunrise 04/27/1991
Sunset 04/17/2011

"Let's Celebrate Life Through Praise"

I am the resurrection and the life; whoever believes in me, even if he dies, will live, and everyone who lives and believes in me will never die. John 11:25

Kayla P. Nimer

"It Was Necessary"

I read a post today that said, "Grief doesn't only show up when we lose a loved one, it's also likely to emerge when we realize we're no longer the same person we were before we started healing." Other scenarios could be when we finally feel safe, when we have outgrown friendships, when we are feeling joy for the first time in a while, when we begin to want different things than we once did, or when we enter a new stage of life.

As we get older, we learn that life is full of losses, it is also full of gains, but one thing we realize as we mature is that some of those losses are inevitable and most of those losses are out of our control. So, what do we do when we lose those things that we hold dearest to our hearts? When those things that we worked so hard for go away, or when we lose people that we loved so much? How do we function when those things are gone and all that we once knew looks completely different?

When I think about grief, I think about grieving previous versions of myself. It took a long time for me to get to a place of understanding that the person that I am will continuously evolve over time.

As crazy as it may seem, at times we think that one day we will *arrive* and we long for that moment even unintentionally but are constantly faced with opportunities to elevate in different aspects and chapters of our lives.

Let us go ahead and rip the Band-Aid off. I hate to break it to you sister or brother, but you will never fully look like you did in previous seasons ever again. I know, you often look back at pictures or reflect on memories of how you showed up back then and now maybe life looked better in the opinion of others or maybe even in your opinion as well. You may feel like a lesser version of yourself in some ways because you are unable to handle things the way you did ten years ago or maybe even last year.

This is where grace comes in. You see you have never been exactly, 100%, where you are right now. On the surface, you may look the same with just a couple of minor changes. Maybe you have a few gray hairs, a few smile wrinkles, enhanced your wardrobe, or started a new self-care journey. Even still, I can promise you that you have never been in the same space, at the same time, dealing with the same thing, under the same circumstances in your life that you are right now.

I remember deciding to move from my hometown of Houston, Texas in the fall of 2019. *Fear* was not a word that was in my mind or my vocabulary, only *faith*. Everything I had done the eighteen months before then had been by faith, I might as well have been the poster child for 2 Corinthians 5:7, which in the New King James Version states, "For we walk by faith, not by sight."

God was truly ordering my steps and I was operating in what Pastor Mike Todd would call, "crazy faith." My life was full of opportunities where my discipline, obedience, and willingness to surrender were constantly being tested. To some, it seemed crazy to leave the life that I had worked so hard to create for myself during my obedience season, but for me, I knew God wanted more out of me. I knew God wanted to stretch me and that it would take a certain level of discomfort for me to become who He needed me to be.

What I did not know was that my life would look completely different, I did not know that I would not show up as that confident person that I was in Houston when I arrived in Dallas. Instead, I arrived like a fly on the wall, a new kid on the block; a student's first day at a new school. Nobody knew what I had done, nobody knew what I was capable of, nobody knew anything about me, not my successes nor my failures.

I had to start to have some serious time being still in total solitude and with my thoughts to discover and explore who I was. I remember thinking, "Now that nobody knows what I've done, what should I do? Who is the person I want to show up as and does she look like how I showed up previously, and if she does not look like her... am I okay with that?"

I started to explore an endless list of questions I never thought to ask myself before, and my answers were all over the place. I had to understand that most of those questions would not be answered because they were not simply up to me, it was up to God. He was the author, writing the words to the various chapters of my life and I was just living the pages.

I had to allow myself time to go through the journey. At times it was hard because I felt so removed from that strong confident established woman that I once was. For a while I found myself starving to get back to her, missing her, wondering when or how I lost her while traveling down a rabbit hole. Then one day, I woke up, and I had a sense of peace. "I am aligned, and I am exactly where God needs me to be!"

I had to say it aloud to confirm my belief in the words God was giving to me. I continued, "I am having the conversations God wants me to have. I am going deeper into healing things that He needed me to heal. I am addressing traumas that He meant for me to address. Prayers that I prayed ten years ago will be answered as a product of my surrender and submission to His will and His way. Even amid uncertainty, I will trust the Lord because He is the head of my life."

Easier said than done right? I would have to write a whole book to tell you every detail of the last thirty-six months of my life, but I will try my best to summarize what I feel will be the most necessary for you as a reader. The journey of dying to my old self, was it always beautiful? No, it was ugly as hell if I must say. There were times I was broken down into the most fragile and delicate parts of me. Times I wanted to throw in the towel, when there was not even a glimpse of light at the end of the tunnel.

Oh, but what you can do with the faith of a mustard seed? Not to mention doing it alone most of the time. Doing it scared and afraid. Now, at thirty-one almost thirty-two years old, I am thankful and filled with so much gratitude for all of those times I felt helpless. For the journey that stripped me naked spiritually but built me back up in a new way. I do not even think to try to compare who I am to who I was, because according to Romans 8:18 of the New International Version, "I consider that our present sufferings are not worth comparing with the glory that will be revealed in us."

I don't have to compare myself to who I used to be because for one I'm not competing with myself, and maybe to some I may have looked stronger or better in previous versions of myself, but even though it took me some time to believe it, I am the very best version of me in this season and for me, that's all that matters.

So, to that person, who is grieving what, who, or where they used to be, my encouragement to you is for you to "Let it go!" Gospel artist, Dewayne Woods, sings a song called, "Let Go" and the chorus says:

As soon as I stop worrying,
Worrying how the story ends,
I let go and I let God,
Let God have His way.

That's when things start happening,
When I stopped looking at back then,

I let go and I let God,
Let God have his way.

God has grace for you, but once you surrender you unlock a whole new level of spiritual alignment. We have to be willing to let go of who we were, to become who we are, and then to evolve into who we are called to be. Sometimes that takes peeling off layers. The very layers that may have been created to survive previous adversities or hardships you faced during a specific period of your life. But these layers will no longer work in this current place of life that you are in.

I am thankful for the grace that was produced from my grief and now when I think about all that I have lost, I choose to acknowledge it in a healthier way by choosing to cherish the moments I was blessed to experience in that period of my life. Moments that helped to shape me into the woman I am today, and then I am met with the feeling of hope and joy because I know that even with all the pressing, molding, breaking, rebuilding, and shaping God has done, He's just getting started.

This is just the beginning, and as Romans 8:28 (NIV) states, "And we know that in all things God works for the good of those who love him, who have been called according to his purpose." I know that God is doing a great work in you the same way He has in me. So go out there and continue to have a heart posture for continuous surrender and keep making those old versions of you proud.

In closing, sometimes what was lost was necessary to push you through the "*growing pains that produced glorious gains*" in your life. Remember as God addresses parts of you that may be hindering you from your elevation, that what God has for you is for you and it can never leave you.

"For the gifts and the calling of God are irrevocable [for He does not withdraw what He has given, nor does He change His mind about those to whom He gives His grace or to whom He sends His call]." Romans 11:29 (AMP)

Kayla P. Nimer

"For me, becoming isn't about arriving somewhere or achieving a certain aim. I see it instead as forward motion, a means of evolving, a way to reach continuously toward a better self. The journey doesn't end." – Michelle Obama, Becoming

Kritina Mock-Palmer

"From Pain to Purpose"

Because I was experiencing so much pain in my life, I couldn't find my purpose. I was sad for many years because of the emotional abuse that I experienced as a child and the mental and physical abuse that I experienced as an adult. The pain of the abuse blinded me from my purpose because I didn't know my worth and I could not see myself. I always felt like I was the black sheep of the family, which as I knew the black sheep was the one no one liked or wanted to be around. The black sheep was an outcast and feeling like the black sheep made me feel alone.

For many years I tried to figure out why I was sad and depressed. I ask myself all the time, how did I survive this state of being, or should I say merely existing? I did not realize the power of my survival skills until I had to use them. When I was down in the valley, I developed the skill of being an overcomer. Isolation helped to shape my perception of who God created me to be. Being alone fine-tuned my ability to hear God's voice. I learned more about myself that I had covered up through pain than I was willing to accept.

Emotional abuse caused me to shut down and hide from my true happiness. The abuse started at an early age by someone who was supposed to love me. I was called black, ugly, and bumpy face so much that I tried to hide because I believed it. I hid behind my grades and sports. I always got good grades and took honor classes, so when I got good grades, I was praised and that helped me escape the pain of being called out of my name. I excelled in sports which made people speak well of me.

I never heard anyone call my sisters ugly and black, so I hid behind their beauty. I would always say I had two light-skinned sisters who looked like twins to shift the focus on them because they were beautiful and not me. I avoided taking pictures. I was more reserved and quieter during my younger years because I felt if I wasn't heard no one would see me.

During my high school years, I was mentally abused by someone whom I thought I was in love with. At first, it was just a friendship, but I fell in love with him, but the feelings were not mutual. He talked down on me, making me feel unloved and unwanted. One day a loved one told me that the young man did not want me because I was black and ugly. This was a trigger based on what I had been told the majority of my life, and it caused me to feel depressed again.

As time went on, he continued to show that he did not want me. After high school, I could not shake the love I felt for him. We only spent time together when no one was around. When we were around others, I was ignored and talked about. Mentally that weighed on me and propelled me into a dark place. I attempted suicide at the age of nineteen. I felt so lost and confused. I began counseling but became angry because it made me face the dark place that I was trying to escape. I stopped going to counseling and tried to handle it on my own.

Life continued and I became pregnant with my first son. It is sad to say, but I was mentally abused again. While pregnant with my second and third son I was in a physically abusive relationship for about four years. I remember getting choked, spat in my face, cut in my head and on my left arm, and having a gun put to my head.

Again, I was being abused by someone who was supposed to love me. Physical abuse caused me to become even more angry and bitter. I was confused as to why I was going through so much abuse. I didn't know how to handle the abuse so I hid the abuse from others as much as I could. I couldn't deal with my pain because I was trying to stay strong and focus on my children. While staying focused on my children, I lost myself, but I kept it hidden well.

After all the abuse and mistreatment, I met Derrick Palmer in March of 2000 and he cared for and loved me with all my scars, pain and hurt, plus he accepted my three sons as his own. On March 31, 2021, I became his wife. During my pregnancies of my fourth son and my only biological daughter, I was loved and protected by him.

Yet, although I was in a great relationship and marriage, I would become angry and bitter thinking of the previous abuse. I didn't want to deal with the pain or even face it, but I couldn't seem to let it go. There were times that I did not like myself because I thought I was the cause of all the pain that was happening to me. I was now a mother of five and a wife of a wonderful man, but I still felt empty.

Don't get me wrong, the love and presence of my children gave me the strength to keep going. But even though life was good, I was still hiding behind my pain. I hid it well by being who I was or so I thought.

My pain caused me to hurt others. There were times that I didn't want to be around my family because I thought they would see my pain and abuse. It was also a time when my family did not want me around because I was so bitter and hateful. I was no longer invited or included in family events. I was sad and alone. Over time, I began to build up hate in my heart. As time went on I did not like how the pain made me feel and I knew then it was time for a change.

As years went on the pain made me think about my life and what I truly wanted. In 2016, I had a choice to either stay in a dark place or rise out of it. I stopped looking at who I was because I knew deep down inside that God had more for me. I was ready to take off the mask and see who I was becoming. I got into my bible more and studied the word. I was raised in church, but I did not have a relationship with God. I chose to serve God and develop a closer relationship with Him.

Prayer became the weapon that I used to fight the pain I was hiding inside. I began to see changes slowly happen in my life. I knew then that prayer was my strongest weapon against pain. I could not fight this battle alone, so I had to call on the Holy Spirit. For the next couple of years, I still found myself in this painful battle where I was suffering in silence. I just wouldn't give this battle to God. I was still trying to figure things out on my own in my own way.

My way would work one day and upset me the next. I would be in the valley one day, and then I would shut some people out of my life and then I would become angry with myself again. With much prayer and fasting, in 2018 I found myself. I forgave myself. I stopped grieving me, and I let go of the pain. I was afraid of opening up about me because of what people would say but I realized that I was holding myself hostage in my own pain.

After forty-six years it was time to face the pain. I knew then that holding on to the pain was going to hold me back from walking in my purpose. Gradually over the next five years, I began doing the work that would produce changes. My purpose was to discover who I was because God has given me the power to be the best me that He called me to be. I found that I love big, and I love hard. Not realizing it, years before I figured it out, my loved one who had gone to be with the lord saw greatness in me and poured so much love into me.

I had to grieve for five special people.

My Aunt Florine Wheatfall-Wesley who loved me unconditionally.

My daddy, JT Mock, encouraged me to be the best version of myself.

My stepdaddy OC Sargent pushed me to become an outstanding entrepreneur.

My godfather Robert Williams encouraged me to not give up on my dreams, and my sister friend.

Tammy Franklin-Curry inspired me to forgive others and showed me how to love people despite what they have done to me.

I then had to properly bury the pain before I was able to move forward in my purpose. Thankfully, I was blessed with Derrick, a strong husband, who went through some of the dark days with me. He loved and prayed with and for me. What is most rewarding is that he stayed with me and never left my side. I had people in my life to love me through my pain and each one played a significant part in teaching me how to overcome it.

Although I didn't learn as quickly as I should have, I learned when it was time. So, all the pain and abuse that I survived pushed me to my purpose. I knew who I was while in pain and I know who I am after the release of the pain. I didn't know how much power I was carrying so I let the pain control my power. I now know that whatever pain or abuse I experienced, God strategically set it up for me to go through it and for me to arise victorious. I took back my power!!

I woke up one morning around 3 am and I began to pray for myself to be released from my pain. After I prayed, all I could say was, "I AM SHE." I just kept repeating to myself, "I AM SHE." To avoid waking anyone up, I began to write:

"She hurt, she was in pain, she cried, she lied, she was unforgiving, she was bitter, she was mistreated, she was abused...But then she prayed, she laughed, she was determined, she forgave, she overcame, and she Loved...Who is she? I AM SHE."

I wanted everyone to see who I AM and not who I WAS!

It took me forty-six years to see the power in me. I have a purpose to love, motivate, inspire, encourage, help, and make a positive impact on people's lives. When I find myself helping others it brings happiness to me.

The greatest thing about finding my purpose was that I was able to see others as I saw myself and I would understand that hurt people do hurt people, so I had to take them differently, not personally. I had to forgive those that I felt brought pain to me because the pain is what birth my purpose. I appreciate the hurt because it healed me. I am glad that my life was a mess because it is now a message to help others.

As I mentioned earlier, I was against counseling. At nineteen, I did not understand that counseling could help me. I felt at that age it was just me telling someone my business. In 2020, at the age of forty-eight, I went back to counseling, and it was a great help to me. I covered up so much of my pain and walked around for years with this mask on. Although I was loved by my husband, my children, and my grandchildren, I still had the fear of being unwanted and unloved.

It was okay for me to have those feelings, but it wasn't okay for me to hold on to them as long as I did and use them as an excuse to be rude to others. I went through two years of setting myself free. In 2022, some of the relationships that were broken were restored. I forgave some people that caused me pain and some people forgave me for the pain that I caused. I had to take accountability for the role I played in the pain and abuse.

So, understand that you can't change what you don't face, and you can't fully walk in your purpose if you don't know what your purpose is. You must know who you are to know what your purpose is and once you know what it is, you must understand why.

Don't fall victim to your pain, claim victory over your pain. Everything that I went through was a process and I had to go through all of it to see the full change in my life. The process isn't always pretty or easy, but it is necessary. When life hits you with many obstacles, don't give up. We are designed to stay in the fight and TRUST THE PROCESS!

I knew God had a plan for me and my life when I was given some of the toughest battles and survived them all. I encourage you with a familiar passage of scripture found in Jeremiah 29:11, "For I know the plans I have for you, declares the Lord, plans for welfare and not for evil, to give you a future and a hope."

In Loving Memory

J.T. Mock

OC Sargent

Tammy Franklin-Curry

Robert Williams

Florine Wheatfall-Wesley

Florine ~ "Thank you for your Loving me."

Tammy ~ "Thank you for your Guiding me."

JT Mock ~ "Thank you for Believing in me."

OC ~ "Thank you for Encouraging me."

Robert ~ "Thank you for Supporting me."

"He heals the brokenhearted and binds up their wounds" Psalm 147:3

Meet The Authors

Kimberly Peterson

Is a Texas native who has a passion for advocating for women's empowerment and has dedicated herself to breaking barriers and fostering inclusivity. At the young age of 22, she embarked on a journey to honor her late mother's memory and restore her legacy by establishing a nonprofit organization.

The Sonia D. Peterson Foundation was born with the primary objectives of educating the community about the importance of regular screenings for diseases, raising awareness about cancer, and emphasizing the critical role of early detection.

Kimberly's journey is a shining example of how one person's passion and determination can create a ripple effect of positive change. As she continues to advocate for women's empowerment and fight against cancer, her impact will undoubtedly be felt for years to come.

Kimberly has recently won an award for Women Who Lead in Nonprofit for efforts to serve the community through The Sonia D. Peterson Foundation.

Contact Information

IG: Kimmypkorner

Email: kimmypkorner@gmail.com

Ashley Arrington

Is a compassionate and dedicated individual, who serves as the CEO/Founder of AGAPE GLOBAL, a transformative organization that has been actively working to improve the lives of the homeless for over five years.

With a deep commitment to ministry outreach and community service, Ashley leads AGAPE GLOBAL in their mission to feed the homeless and bring hope to individuals in need.

Her unwavering passion and dedication to serving others drive her to find innovative ways to support the homeless community and uplift those who need it most through AGAPE GLOBAL's impactful initiatives. Through the power of compassion, outreach, and service, Ashley Arrington continues to make a difference in the lives of the homeless and inspire others to join in the pursuit of a brighter future.

Contact Information

Facebook: @Ashley Arrington

IG: @elevated_ashley18

TikTok: @elevated_ashley18

Email: Agapeglobal19@gmail.com

LaTeshia Bailey

Is a Native Houstonian who has worked as a business professional in the financial industry for over 20 years. She's helped thousands of clients throughout her career reach their financial goals by helping them navigate through the different stages of life. She considers her faith in God and her relationship with her family and close friends to be most valuable to her.

She is a proud mother of a handsome, well-mannered, and loving son, who is the light of her life along with her "Angel Baby", a daughter, who is in Heaven, whom she misses daily. LaTeshia has faced many of life's challenges growing up but more intensely during the onset of the global pandemic.

These experiences led her to a passion for coaching and helping women maneuver through the multiple stages of grief and coping. Her goal is to mentor women who have withstood separation, divorce, the loss of an unborn child, and abandonment. While using strategic coping mechanisms she attains to help women identify their purpose and true identity.

Contact Information

IG: Ladytb007

Simone Gooden

Is a Native Houstonian, who is a diligent and highly motivated laboratory and corporate professional, drawing upon ten years of experience in healthcare contributing to smooth and productive operations.

Simone is a lifelong learner, always finding ways to grow and evolve in this changing world. She is a graduate of Texas Southern University, earning her bachelor's degree of science in Clinical Laboratory Science. She also recently received her master's degree from Louisiana State University Shreveport in Health Administration. She has a passion for science and works in the healthcare field as a microbiologist.

When she is not working, she enjoys spending time with family and friends. She is an avid traveler and sports enthusiast who enjoys cooking and reading. She is thankful to God for guiding her steps along the way and will continue to lead with love and compassion as she progresses to accomplish her dreams.

Contact Information

Facebook: @Simone Gooden

IG: @ _simplymonie_

Email: simone.gooden23@gmail.com

Natarsha Hackney

Is a creative, outgoing, and down-to-earth individual with a passion for art and a love for socializing and meeting new people. She is always seeking inspiration from the world around her. As an aspiring artist, she dreams of exploring various artistic mediums and leaving a unique mark on the world.

Whether it's drawing, painting, sculpting, or other expressive avenues, Natarsha is always ready to dive in headfirst. Having traveled extensively for work, her experiences with that have shaped her perspective and fueled a desire to see even more of the world.

With a vibrant personality and imaginative spirit, she is on a journey to produce, connect, and make a lasting impact. With faith and patience, her life has finally taken the journey she has been praying for.

Contact Information

Email: hackneyn@yahoo.com

Lisa Johnson Ade-Oni

Is a loving mother and wife from Bay City, Texas. My Doctoral studies are in Psychology and Social Criminal Justice. I am a motivational speaker who represents memberships to several suicide awareness organizations and affiliated organizations.

I have specialized in servicing mentally challenged individuals for the past 10 years and am the owner of Bukoba Trucking Company.

My pleasure in life is traveling around the world, especially to Nigeria and Ghana Africa to support several orphanages I have built and oversee several water wells I have donated to the villages of Africa. Giving back is my passion in life.

Contact Information

Facebook: @lisa.l.johnson

TikTok: @lisasly2019

Snapchat: @jazziediva49

Kayla Nimer

Is a national community engagement manager by day but is most known as a daughter, friend, faithful servant, woman of faith, spoken-word artist, moderator, and "The Elevation Plug". She is the owner and founder of The Elevation Plug, a network created to help minorities address their hinderances and elevate personally and professionally. She is also the host of "The Plug Effect LIVE Podcast."

She has responded to the call on her life to push people to their divine purpose and to show people through her testimony and transparency that they have the power to overcome any adversity through faith, discipline, and most importantly obedience. "No matter what hand you've been dealt in life, you can still play a good game and you can still win" is her motto and she walks boldly in it.

Contact Information

Facebook: @ kaylaprincessn

IG: @ kaylapnimer

Kritina Mock-Palmer

Is a woman of faith, who puts God first in everything she does. Her experiences with abuse, neglect, and mistreatment, have driven her to make it her mission to encourage, inspire, and motivate women from all walks of life. She desires to be an example of a woman who overcomes obstacles and struggles. She has worked hard to become Strong and Successful.

Kritina obtained her associate degree from Blinn College in Medical Office Management and a certificate in Business Management. She attended Sam Houston State University and studied Criminal Justice and Psychology. She worked in the medical field for over 10 years. And has been working in the childcare industry for over 15 years and is the proud owner of NeNe's Child Care Center LLC. I am also the owner of I AM SHE, LLC for five years. I am a wife of 23 years, mother of five biological and three by marriage, and grandmother of six.

Contact Information

Facebook: @ Kritina LaNee Mock-Palmer

IG: @mocktena

Email: iamshekmp@gmail.com

Made in the USA
Columbia, SC
23 May 2024